Literature Log

A Place to Note What You Notice

HEINEMANN
Portsmouth, NH

Heinemann
361 Hanover Street
Portsmouth, NH 03801–3912
www.heinemann.com

Offices and agents throughout the world

ISBN-13: 978-0-325-05666-1

Editor: Debra Doorack
Production: Patricia Adams
Cover and interior designs: Lisa Fowler and Monica Ann Crigler
Typesetter: Eclipse Publishing Services
Manufacturing: Steve Bernier

Printed in the United States of America on acid-free paper
17 16 15 14   VP   3 4 5

About the Authors

This literature log was created by **Kylene Beers** and **Robert Probst**. They are both former teachers—Dr. Beers in middle school and Dr. Probst in high school—and both have spent time at universities teaching folks who want to become teachers. They've also coauthored a book for teachers titled *Notice and Note: Strategies for Close Reading*. In fact, you probably have this book in your hands because your teacher read *Notice and Note*.

If the literature book you use in your language arts class was published by a company called Holt Rinehart Winston, or Holt McDougal, or Houghton Mifflin Harcourt, then look at who the authors are because there's a good chance that you'll see either or both of their names on that author page. And if you ask your teacher, you might find that your teacher has read other books by Dr. Beers or Dr. Probst or that your teacher has watched one of their educational videos on YouTube or follows them on Twitter. That's because both Dr. Beers and Dr. Probst work in many different ways to help teachers connect you and other kids just like you to books and reading.

Dr. Probst lives in the Florida Keys, where he enjoys scuba diving when he's not working. Dr. Beers lives right outside of Houston, Texas, where she enjoys taking cooking classes and working in her garden. Both of them love to read and are often found in schools across the country helping kids become better readers.

Contents

List titles of books or short stories you're reading here.

STOP!

Read These Terribly Important and Cannot-Skip Two Pages First!

In 2013 we published a book for teachers titled *Notice and Note: Strategies for Close Reading.* Its purpose was to give your teacher some ideas for helping you—yes, you!—read better. No, we don't really know who you are, but we know you're a student. We know that you probably like to do a lot of different things, and for some of you that includes reading, while others of you might not see yourselves as readers.

We also know that *we* read every single day. We read emails and text messages. We read articles about teaching. We read books about helping kids become better readers and books about cooking and scuba diving. We read letters and advertisements and newspapers, and we read novels. We read all sorts of novels—historical fiction, science fiction, and realistic fiction. Some are short; some are long. Some we loved reading and some, well, some we read because we had to even though we didn't like them very much.

We know that reading is critical. It not only is a great way to be entertained, but it's our major source of learning something new. Yes, we can learn things by listening to a teacher, watching TV, or watching a YouTube clip, but reading about something is often the best way to learn about it.

But is reading fiction REALLY important?

Yes! We think some of the most important lessons we have ever learned have come from reading fiction. It's in these fictional stories that we've learned about ourselves and others. Lessons about how important it is to be a good friend; to be an honest person; to remember that even when we lose someone we love a lot, that dear one is still with us in our memories. When we read *The Hunger Games* we learned about courage; when we read *Harry Potter* we learned about making tough choices; when we read *Wonder* we learned about what it means to be a good friend. And with each book, we learned more about ourselves.

So, how did we get ALL those important lessons from those books?

Well, we didn't learn those lessons because the authors of those books put in a note that said, "Here's an important lesson. Learn this!" No. We learned those lessons because we both know how to read a text closely. We know how to look for some things that we call *signposts*. These signposts help us understand how characters are changing, how conflicts are being resolved, and ultimately, what theme—or lesson—the author is trying to convey. And we know that you, too, can learn to be a reader who notices these signposts and uses them to help you understand character development, internal conflict, and theme.

You can use the *Notice and Note Literature Log* to practice noticing those signposts and to keep a log or a record of the ones you see in the books you are reading. Use the signposts you find to help you have smart conversations about your books and to provide the evidence you'll need to support the points you want to make when you write about these books. This log is divided into three sections:

> **Part One:** The Signposts
> **Part Two:** My Reading Record
> **Part Three:** My Book Notes

In Part One, you'll get some information about each signpost and some passages you can read to practice noticing the signposts. Your teacher will probably tell you much more about these signposts than you'll find here.

In Part Two, you'll find a sample reading record and a blank one you can use to keep a record of some books you read this year.

In Part Three, you'll find many pages in which you can keep notes about the books you read. It's in this section that we want you to keep a record of the signposts you notice and what you think each signpost means. You'll also find pages in this section where you can take notes and record vocabulary words. And, of course, this is your log, so add thoughts of your own that you don't want to lose.

What we hope happens with YOU and this log this year

Mostly, though, this log exists to help you become a closer reader. That's what we really want. We want you to find some books you love, and we want you to love the lessons you discover in them. We want you to meet characters who become good friends. We want you to stay up late (well, not too late) reading something you just can't stop reading. We want you to become a reader who notices much as you read.

Part **One**

The Signposts

This section is a place for you to take notes about the signposts your teacher shares with you. Throughout this section you'll see some charts that Ms. Ochoa, a teacher in New York City, made to hang on her classroom walls. They are there to remind her students to be alert for the signposts as they read. Your teacher might have made similar charts for your classroom.

We also like the chart that you see here. It gives you a quick overview of all of the signposts that you'll be learning about!

The Signposts

My Notes About
Contrasts and Contradictions

Practice Noticing: **Contrasts and Contradictions**

You will never find a book or a story without a Contrasts and Contradiction signpost. If you did, it would probably be so dull that you wouldn't read more than a few pages before giving up on it entirely. You want to see something happen that *contrasts* with what you would have expected. And you want to see someone behave in a way that is different from—that *contradicts*—the way he or she has been acting.

This signpost surprises us with something unexpected, but we have to be alert for it. And—just as important—we have to stop and think about what it means. When the writer gives us this signpost, he's letting us know that here is a clue to something important. It's as if he's saying, "This passage doesn't solve the mystery for you, but it's a clue that will help *you* figure things out."

Quick Tip

When you read something in social studies or history class, you will need to change the anchor question to "Why would the people act this way?" or "Why would the government act this way?"

So when you spot a contrast or a contradiction, stop and ask yourself a simple question: *Why is the character acting this way?*

Here's an example. You have a friend who has sat beside you at the cafeteria table at lunch every day of the school year so far. She eats her peanut butter and jelly sandwich, you eat your Swiss cheese and turkey, and then you both go off to your next class. But what if, today, you came into the cafeteria, sat down, and spotted her at a table in the far corner? You would certainly notice that, and you would say to yourself, "I wouldn't have expected her to be over there instead of right here where she usually is." You'd say that because her behavior on this day *contrasts* with what you would have predicted, that it *contradicts* the pattern she has followed for the whole year. And so you would wonder, "Why is she acting this way?"

That contradictory behavior was a clue that something has changed. Authors show us change with contrasts and contradictions, too. For instance, take a look at Passage 1.

Passage 1

Here is an example of Contrasts and Contradictions from a book we both like, *The Watsons Go to Birmingham—1963*, by Christopher Paul Curtis. At one point in this book, we see that the main character, Kenny, is thinking about something mean that his older brother, Byron, just did. Kenny calls Byron a nickname, Daddy Cool.

> Leave it to Daddy Cool to kill a bird, then give it a funeral. Leave it to Daddy Cool to torture human kids at school all day long and never have his conscience bother him but to feel sorry for a stupid little grayish brown bird. (p. 84)

What Did You Notice?

Reread those two sentences and underline the part that makes you think of a contrast or a contradiction. Then, in the blanks below, answer the anchor question, *Why do you think the character—Daddy Cool—acts that way?* Reading both sentences will help you answer that question.

_____

_____

_____

_____

_____

_____

Here's What We Noticed

> Leave it to Daddy Cool <u>to kill a bird, then give it a funeral</u>. Leave it to Daddy Cool to torture human kids at school all day long and never have his conscience bother him but to feel sorry for a stupid little grayish brown bird. (p. 84)

Mrs. Beers saw this as a C&C.

From Dr. Beers: When I read these two sentences, I thought that killing a bird and then giving it a funeral was an interesting contradiction. And then when Kenny pointed out that Daddy Cool tortures kids all day but feels sorry for a little bird, I knew I was seeing real contradictions in how Daddy Cool—Byron—acted. When I asked myself, "Why would Byron act this way?" I had to admit I wasn't sure, but I realized that there must be some part of Byron that is good or he wouldn't want to give the bird a funeral. That helped me realize that the author is showing me that Byron isn't all bad, that he has a tender side.

From Dr. Probst: I agree. Byron's behavior is confusing. At one point he kills a bird, but then he gives it a funeral. His brother points out that he tortures kids at school but seems upset about a dead bird. I think the author shows us this contradictory behavior to help us realize that there's more to Byron than being a bully. I'll watch to see how his character develops through the rest of the story.

Passage 2

Here's another contrast and contradiction that we spotted in another book, *The Giver*, by Lois Lowry. In this example, the contrast and contradiction appears suddenly in just one sentence as a character called The Giver does something. Read the sentence and underline what you see as the contradiction, and then in the blanks below, answer the anchor question, *Why does the character act this way?*

> The Giver smiled, though his smile was oddly harsh. (p. 105)

_____

_____

_____

_____

_____

_____

Here's What We Noticed

From both of us: To be honest with you, the two of us never saw a contrast or contradiction in this sentence! It was Mark, a ninth grader from South Carolina, who pointed it out.

From Mark: I stopped here because I noticed how it said he had a harsh smile. Smiles aren't harsh.

From both of us: Wow! Mark is right—smiles are supposed to show that one is happy. In this case, the author obviously wants us to realize that The Giver has contradictory feelings. He's smiling on the outside but not feeling that way on the inside. Mark went on:

From Mark: I noted that because it was really a contradiction, and I wondered why he would be sad and smiling. I think that The Giver is smiling because he's still trying to make Jonas feel good about this assignment, but he also knows something that Jonas doesn't know. This part made me think that something important is finally going to happen that's about Jonas finding out something.

Quick Tip

Contrasts and contradictions usually help us understand how characters are changing. When you talk about the contrasts and contradictions that you noticed, you might use phrases such as "this shows me some interesting character development. . . ."

From both of us: Now, as you thought about the anchor question—*Why would The Giver act that way?*—you didn't have enough information in front of you from that one sentence to have all the detail that Mark gave us. But we hope you realized that smiles aren't supposed to be harsh. They should be happy. This might make you think that The Giver isn't happy about something but must pretend that he is.

What's critical to notice, though, is that a contrast and contradiction can be found in a single sentence.

STOP and Notice & Note

Aha Moment

When you're reading and suddenly a character realizes, understands, or finally figures something out, you should stop and ask yourself:

"How might this change things?"

If the character figured out a problem, you probably just learned about the conflict.

If the character understood a life lesson, you probably just learned the theme.

My Notes About
Aha Moment

Practice Noticing: **Aha Moment**

When we notice characters pointing out what they have realized, then we know the author is showing us how they are changing—an Aha Moment. Those changes usually mean the plot will shift in some way. That's why the anchor question for this signpost—*How might this change things?*—is important. The question reminds us to pause and consider how what the characters have figured out might affect what they think or do next.

It's usually easy to spot an Aha Moment because authors may have characters use phrases such as "I understood" or "I realized" or "I finally knew" or "it suddenly occurred to me" as the signal that they have figured something out. Take a look at these sentences from several different books to see what we mean. It doesn't matter if you don't know the books; we just want you to see how easy it is to notice this signpost. Underline the words that signal to you that the character has realized something.

> Now she knew for certain what Uncle Henrik had meant when he had talked to her in the barn. To be brave came more easily if you knew nothing. (From *Number the Stars*, by Lois Lowry, p. 84)

> For the first time, it occurred to me that maybe my mother's leaving had nothing whatsoever to do with me. (From *Walk Two Moons*, by Sharon Creech, p. 176)

> And having you here with me over the past year has made me realize that things must change. For years I've thought they should, but it seemed hopeless. (From *The Giver*, by Lois Lowry, pp. 154–155)

We wonder which words you marked. In the first example, we would have underlined *knew* or *knew for certain*. In the second, we would have marked *occurred* or perhaps "For the first time it occurred to me. . . ." And in the third example, we would have marked *realize* or "made me realize that things must change." Now, try this with a longer passage.

Passage 1

This passage is from *Esperanza Rising*, by Pamela Muñoz Ryan. Here, the main character, Esperanza, is inside after working in the fields all day. This is new work for her, since until recently her family had lived a very comfortable life and she never had to do hard work. Here Esperanza is trying something that might make her hands soft, the way they once were.

> She put her hands under the faucet, rinsed off the avocado, and patted them dry. They felt better, but still looked red and weathered. She took another avocado, cut it in half, swung the knife into the pit and pulled it from the flesh. She repeated Hortensia's recipe and as she sat for the second time with her hands smothered, she realized that it wouldn't matter how much avocado and glycerine she put on them, they would never look like the hands of a wealthy woman from El Rancho de las Rosas. Because they were the hands of a poor campesina. (pp. 181–182)

What Did You Notice?

Reread that passage and underline the signpost that shows you the aha moment. Then, in the space below, see if you can answer the anchor question, *How might this change things?* Since you haven't read the 180 pages that came before this passage, you'll have to read this one paragraph closely to think about what Esperanza's realization might mean. You might come up with several ideas.

_____

_____

_____

_____

Here's What We Noticed

From Dr. Beers: We bet you quickly saw that word *realized* and underlined it. Or maybe you underlined the phrase "she realized that it wouldn't matter."

From Dr. Probst: Aha Moments are usually very easy to spot. The trickier part is thinking about what they mean. In this passage, I think that Esperanza has suddenly realized that being wealthy isn't a part of her future. Since she was doing the avocado treatment to get her hands soft, realizing that they won't ever be soft again might be a disappointment for her.

From Dr. Beers: I agree. And as I read this passage I saw another signpost, and it was this other signpost that helped me understand how disappointed she is with her realization. Look back to the passage and see if you can spot what I saw . . .

Quick Tip

Often, when you notice an Aha Moment there will be another signpost nearby. Sometimes that's Contrasts and Contradictions and other times it might be Memory Moment or Tough Questions. Be alert and remember that these signposts often show up in pairs.

* * *

From both of us: Did you see that second signpost? The underlined part below is the second signpost that Dr. Beers saw.

> She put her hands under the faucet, rinsed off the avocado, and patted them dry. They felt better, but still looked red and weathered. She took another avocado, cut it in half, swung the knife into the pit and pulled it from the flesh. She repeated Hortensia's recipe and as she sat for the second time with her hands smothered, she realized that it wouldn't matter how much avocado and glycerine she put on them, they would never look like the hands of a wealthy woman from El Rancho de las Rosas. Because they were the hands of a poor campesina. (pp. 181–182)

This is a contrast and contradiction.

She's putting the avocado on her hands so they will look like the hands of a wealthy woman because wealthy women don't have to do hard work in the fields, but she realizes that hers won't look that way because she is poor. This contrast between what she wants and what she is seems to be a problem for Esperanza. We're not sure if this realization will make her work harder to become wealthy again or if it means she has accepted her new position in life. The only way we'll know is to keep reading the book.

Passage 2

Here's another Aha Moment signpost, this time from *The Watsons Go to Birmingham—1963*, by Christopher Paul Curtis. In this passage, Kenny is on a school bus with his friend, Rufus and his younger brother Cody. Rufus and Cody are very poor, and a mean kid, Larry, decides to make fun of the clothes Rufus and Cody wear. After a rude comment from Larry, everyone on the school bus, including Kenny, laughs.

Read the passage below and underline the portion that shows you that Kenny is having an aha moment. Then, in the space below, answer the anchor question, *How might this change things?*

> Maybe it was because everybody else was laughing, maybe it was because Cody had such a strange look on his face while he peeked at his underpants, maybe it was because I was glad that Larry hadn't jumped on me, but whatever the reason was I cracked up too.
>
> Rufus shot a look at me. His face never changed but I knew right away I'd done something wrong. I tried to squeeze the rest of my laugh down. (p. 43)

_____

_____

_____

_____

_____

_____

Here's What We Noticed

From both of us: We marked the words "I knew right away," although just marking *knew* would have been fine, too. Sometimes aha moments occur gradually, over time, but in this case it happened in an instant. Kenny *knew* or realized that laughing was wrong. We think this might mean that he apologizes or that perhaps he stands up to Larry or maybe he just feels guilty. We won't really know until we keep reading.

Quick Tip

On page 10 you may have noticed a line that consists of three asterisks in the middle of the page:

* * *

Look back and find them. What do you think they might be suggesting?

We used them to let you know that we were pausing for you, the reader, to do something. We wanted you to take a few minutes to think about the question we had raised or do what we suggested you do.

All punctuation marks act as little signposts. The asterisks on page 10 are something that you don't see as often as a comma or a period, but they often suggest a break, or a pause, and you should take a moment to stop and think about what you've just read.

STOP and Notice & Note

Tough Questions

When you're reading and the character asks himself a really difficult question,

You should stop and ask yourself:

"What does this question make me wonder about?"

The answers will tell you about the conflict and might give you ideas about what will happen later in the story.

My Notes About
Tough Questions

_____

_____

_____

_____

_____

_____

_____

_____

_____

_____

_____

_____

_____

_____

_____

_____

_____

_____

_____

_____

_____

_____

_____

_____

_____

_____

Practice Noticing: **Tough Questions**

The Tough Questions signpost was one of the first we found when we set out looking for the signposts your teacher has been teaching you. Perhaps we found this signpost early because Tough Questions are so easy to spot! As you read, stay alert for those places in which a character asks himself or a trusted friend questions that are very hard to answer. These questions often reveal some sort of fear or problem that must be faced, and when they do they help us understand the internal conflict that a character is working to overcome or a difficult choice he has to make.

Take a look at this short passage from *Walk Two Moons,* by Sharon Creech.

> Later that afternoon, when Phoebe and I went downstairs, Mrs. Winterbottom was talking with Prudence. "Do you think I lead a tiny life?" she asked. (p. 88)

Even without knowing who these characters are, you can easily see the tough question Mrs. Winterbottom has asked: "Is my life tiny?" Once you see that, you want to consider the anchor question, *What does this question make me wonder about?* We can wonder a lot of things: Has something or someone made her feel as if her life is insignificant? Does this bother her so much that she will try to change something about her life? If that's the case, then we should watch for Mrs. Winterbottom to begin doing things that might surprise us.

Now, let's have you read some passages and look for the tough questions.

Passage 1

This passage is from *Among the Hidden,* by Margaret Haddix. Here, the main character, Luke, is talking with his mother about his older brothers, Matthew and Mark.

> "Matthew and Mark never had to hide, did they?" he asked.
>   Mother was scrubbing the remains of scrambled eggs out of the skillet. She turned her head and looked at him carefully.
>   "No," she said.

"Then why do I?"

"Oh, Lukie, do you really need to know? Isn't it enough to know—things are just different for you?"

He thought about that. . . . She still read bedtime stories to him, and he knew Matthew and Mark thought that was sissified. Was that what she meant? But he was just younger. He'd grow up. Wouldn't he be like them then?

With unusual stubbornness, Luke insisted, "I want to know why I'm different. I want to know why I have to hide." (pp. 8–9)

What Did You Notice?

Reread that passage and underline the tough questions. Then, in the space below, see if you can answer the anchor question, *What does this make me wonder about?* This conversation occurs early in the book, so you'll probably wonder the same things that we did, even though we'd read the previous seven pages.

_____

_____

_____

_____

_____

_____

Here's What We Noticed

From both of us: Tough questions are rather obvious—you just look for the questions that are, well, tough! We selected this passage because we thought you might want to mark a couple of examples.

From Dr. Probst: We think the real tough question in this passage is "Then why do I?" That's the hard one for his mom to answer, and it's what bothers Luke. Because his mom seems reluctant to answer it, we see just how troubling it is.

From Dr. Beers: And you can tell just how important it is to Luke by that final sentence: "With unusual stubbornness, Luke insisted, 'I want to know why I'm different.'" Though he doesn't state it as a question, he's pushing her to answer him.

From Dr. Probst: Plus, did you notice that in that phrase Dr. Beers just mentioned the author gives us another signpost that shows that this is very important to Luke? Look at that phrase, "with unusual stubbornness." Take a moment and think of the other signposts you've learned. What signpost is this? Write your answer below.

_____

_____

Quick Tip

It's not uncommon to see more than one signpost in a passage. In the passage you just read, there's a Contrast and Contradiction. Look back and see if you can spot it! Check your answer with ours by looking on page 18!

From Dr. Beers: Did you recognize this as a Contrast and Contradiction? Since this is "unusual" stubbornness for Luke, he probably seldom behaves this way. *Why would he act this way?* Why is he now stubborn about this? Obviously, this question about hiding is very important.

From both of us: As we thought about Luke's tough questions—and asked ourselves the anchor question, *What does this make me wonder about?*—we began to suspect that hiding is getting harder for him. We wonder if, when he was very young, he didn't realize that he was hiding but now is more and more aware of how different his life is. Since we know that the tough question shows us the internal conflict, we wonder how hiding—and not being happy about that—will shape the book. Perhaps he will decide he no longer wants to hide.

From Dr. Beers: Some of you might have also marked the questions Luke's mom asked him: "Do you really need to know? Isn't it enough to know—things are just different for you?" While we think the tougher question comes from Luke, it's fine if you marked this as a Tough Question if you think she seriously is asking something that reveals a problem she has.

That's what tough questions do. They let you, the reader, inside a character's head to see what his or her main problems are. If you really think this helps you think about the problems the mom faces, then you certainly should mark this as a Tough Question. As a mom, when I see her questions I have to wonder if she doesn't know something that she really doesn't want to tell him. She's hoping he won't push her. The conflict she might feel has to do with finally being honest with her son about something. That could be very tough.

Passage 2

Here's another passage that includes several questions. Read this and underline the questions that you think are tough questions and then answer the anchor question in the blanks below. This is a conversation from *Esperanza Rising*, by Pamela Muñoz Ryan, between Esperanza and her mother.

"Esperanza, if we had stayed in Mexico and I had married Tio Luis, we would have had one choice. To be apart and miserable. Here, we have two choices. To be together and miserable or to be together and happy. . . . I choose to be happy. So which will you choose?"

The weariness from the days of travel flooded over [Esperanza] and her mind wandered from people peeing in ditches, to Marta's rudeness, to the horse stalls at El Rancho de las Rosas.

How could she be grateful when she had never been more miserable in her life? (pp. 104–106)

_____

_____

_____

_____

_____

_____

Here's What We Noticed

From both of us: We saw two important questions, "So which will you choose?" and "How could she be happy or grateful when she had never been more miserable in her life?" Both of these questions made us wonder if Esperanza isn't a little selfish. Her mother is pointing out something very important—that they are still together—and yet Esperanza isn't able to focus on that. She's focusing on things such as someone being rude. The mom's question—"So which will you choose?"—reminds us that happiness is something we create by controlling how we feel inside. At this point, Esperanza seems more concerned about things around her and not feelings inside of her.

We also noticed another signpost as we read this passage. If you didn't spot it, reread.

* * *

The other signpost we noticed is Contrasts and Contradictions. This time, the contrast is between how Esperanza's mother feels and how Esperanza feels. One chooses to be happy, while the other seems to choose to be sad. When we ask ourselves how Esperanza's mom could feel this way, we realize that she values family more than things; Esperanza, by contrast, still seems focused on things. Seeing this contrast confirms that, at this point, Esperanza is self-centered.

Quick Tip

Occasionally you'll see a Tough Questions signpost not written as a question but instead as a "wonder" statement such as this: "She wondered if life would ever be the same." Treat these wonder statements the same as Tough Questions because they too are revealing an inner fear or worry.

Quick Tip

Our answer to the question we asked in the Quick Tip on page 16 is the phrase: "with unusual stubbornness." Normally Luke isn't stubborn, but now he is. Obviously hiding bothers him.

STOP and Notice & Note

Words of the Wiser

When you're reading and a character (who's probably older and lots wiser) takes the main character aside and gives serious advice,

You should stop and ask yourself:

"What's the life lesson, and how might it affect the character?"

Whatever the lesson is, you've probably found a theme for the story.

My Notes About
Words of the Wiser

Practice Noticing: **Words of the Wiser**

When we started our search to identify these six signposts we identified this one last. But that doesn't mean it isn't one of the most valuable ones! As your teacher explained, when you notice a character sharing wise words—what some might call a *life lesson*—you'll be seeing an important idea that the author wants you to think about. As you think about that idea, you'll often find yourself thinking about the theme of the book.

Often, Words of the Wiser scenes are part of a long, serious talk between the wiser character and the main character. But in other instances, the Words of the Wiser signpost might appear as a single sentence. That's what happens in this scene from *The Wednesday Wars*, by Gary D. Schmidt, in which a teacher is talking to the main character, a seventh grader named Holling:

> Learn everything you can—everything. And then use all that you have learned to grow up to be a wise and good man. (p. 225)

In this one sentence, the teacher offers Holling some advice he can use his entire life. Then, as we think about the anchor question—*How might this lesson affect the character?*—we realize that perhaps the teacher has shared this advice with Holling because Holling hasn't been trying very hard. Perhaps he hasn't been acting in a wise and good way. We think that this lesson will help him rethink some of his actions and maybe influence something he does later in the book.

Now you try to identify the wise words in the passages below. When you notice a Words of the Wiser signpost, stop and ask yourself, *What's the life lesson, and how might this affect the character?*

Passage 1

The following passage is from *Tuck Everlasting*, by Natalie Babitt. Here, the main character, Winnie, is talking with an older woman named Mae. Mae has told Winnie about her family's tough situation, and Winnie responds by saying . . .

It sounded rather sad to Winnie, never to belong anywhere. "That's too bad," she said, glancing shyly at Mae. "Always moving around and never having any friends."

But Mae shrugged off this observation. "Tuck and me, we got each other," she said, "and that's a lot. The boys, now, they go their separate ways. They're some different, don't always get on too good. But they come home whenever the spirit moves, and every ten years, first week of August, they meet at the spring and come home together so's we can be family again for a little while. . . . One way or another, it all works out." She folded her arms and nodded, more to herself than Winnie. "Life's got to be lived, no matter how long or short," she said calmly. "You got to take what comes. We just go along, like everybody else, one day at a time. Funny— we don't feel no different. Leastways, I don't. Sometimes I forget about what's happened to us, forget it altogether. And then sometimes it comes over me and I wonder why it happened to us. We're plain as salt, us Tucks. We don't deserve no blessings—if it is a blessing. And likewise, I don't see how we deserve to be cursed, if it's a curse. Things just are, and fussing don't bring changes." (pp. 54–55)

What Did You Notice?

Reread that passage and underline the Words of the Wiser signpost. Then, in the space below, see if you can answer the anchor question, *What's the lesson, and how might this affect Winnie?*

_____

_____

_____

_____

_____

Here's What We Noticed

From both of us: We saw two comments that we thought were Words of the Wiser.

From Dr. Probst: The first one I saw was the line "Life's got to be lived, no matter how long or short . . . You got to take what comes." This is an important lesson about not running from your problems, but directly facing what happens to you in life. Since we don't have any other context for this story from this one passage, I don't know if Winnie will remember Mae's advice and follow it when she faces problems.

From Dr. Beers: I saw that lesson, too. I also marked "fussing don't bring changes." I thought this was a very important lesson for Winnie and actually for anyone. Actions change things; whining and fussing don't. From this single passage, we don't know what's happening with Winnie, so I'm not sure why she needs this advice right now. Since we're early in the book, I wonder if Winnie will face a problem in which she could worry and fuss about something or actually do something.

From both of us: You won't be surprised at this: There's another signpost in this passage! Did you notice it? If not, go back and reread.

* * *

From Dr. Beers: We hope that when you reread you saw the "I wonder" statement. Don't forget that sometimes tough questions appear as "I wonder" statements. Mae said, "I wonder why it happened to us." From this one paragraph, we don't know what this "it" is, but it's obviously important because it could be seen as a blessing or a curse. It seems to bother Mae and is obviously something that she can't answer. It's a conflict that Mae, even as an adult, hasn't yet resolved.

Passage 2

Now read this next passage and look for the Words of the Wiser signpost. Underline the advice that is offered and then answer the anchor question in the blanks below. This is a conversation between a father and a daughter, Sal, from a book titled *Walk Two Moons,* by Sharon Creech.

Quick Tip

The Words of the Wiser signpost often appears as a scene just between the main character and the person offering the advice. You'll know you've found a Words of the Wiser signpost when the advice would help the character—and perhaps you, too—throughout all of life.

> "Sal. Your mother went because she wanted to go."
> "We should have stopped her."
> "A person isn't a bird. You can't cage a person."
> "She shouldn't have gone." (p. 141)

_____

_____

_____

_____

_____

_____

Here's What We Noticed

From both of us: When we read this scene, we saw the wise words that the father was offering his daughter, Sal: "You can't cage a person." We think this advice means that people need to be free to make their own choices even if we don't like those choices. We aren't sure how Sal will use this advice, but this scene shows us that Sal is struggling with her mom's choice to leave and perhaps with her dad's willingness to let her leave. Maybe her dad's comment will help her understand why he didn't try to stop her mom.

Quick Tip

Don't be surprised when the advice offered in a Words of the Wiser moment isn't followed! Usually the main character hears the advice but then still does what he wants to do! It's later in the book, sometimes, after the main character has struggled through some problems that he realizes just how wise those words were.

My Notes About
Again and Again

STOP and Notice & Note

Again and Again

When you're reading and you notice a word, phrase, object, or situation mentioned over and over,

You should stop and ask yourself:

"Why does this keep showing up again and again?"

The answers will tell you about the theme and conflict, or they might foreshadow what will happen later.

_____
_____
_____
_____
_____
_____
_____
_____
_____
_____
_____
_____
_____
_____
_____
_____
_____
_____
_____
_____
_____
_____
_____
_____
_____

Practice Noticing: Again and Again

If at the beginning of class your teacher mentions that you might want to reread a certain chapter in a book, and later in class she mentions again that this chapter has very important information, and then at the end of class she says one more time that it would be good to know that chapter, you might want to stop and ask yourself, "So, why is she mentioning this chapter again and again?" If you're astute, you'll realize that she's giving you a hint that you might soon see a quiz on that chapter!

It's human nature to mention important things again and again, and so we shouldn't be surprised when this happens in a book. The author might repeat just one word. For instance, in *The Giver*, by Lois Lowry, the word *release* is used again and again. You can't help but wonder why this one word keeps coming up so often; you know it must mean something important long before you figure out just what that is.

Other times authors might repeat an event. For instance, in a book titled *Roll of Thunder, Hear My Cry*, by Mildred Taylor, a group of black children walking to school down a dirt road get angry when the school bus carrying white children drives past them and covers them with dust. Not too many pages later, the kids are walking to school again and that same school bus comes by and they get covered in dust, again. This time they are angrier. When they start walking to school on another morning, you already know that bus is coming, and you realize that since the kids got angrier the second time, they'll probably get even angrier this time. You realize that something will probably happen. You also begin to see that it really isn't the bus that's the problem; it's that the white kids get to ride the bus while the black kids must walk.

What's hard about noticing Again and Again moments is that what's being repeated might have occurred one page ago or three chapters ago. So you must be alert when you read. And when you do notice something that's happened again and again, be sure to stop and ask yourself, *Why might the author bring this up again and again?*

Passage 1

Here are three scenes from *Riding Freedom*, by Pam Muñoz Ryan. You'll easily spot what's occurring again and again. In the first scene, the main character, Charlotte, is talking with an older character, Vern.

> "I know. I know, Miss Charlotte," said Vern. "You gotta do what your heart tells you." (p. 38)

In this second scene, we find Charlotte remembering Vern's words:

> She could still hear Vern saying, "You gotta do what your heart tells you." (p. 40)

In the third scene, Charlotte returns to Vern's words once again:

> She took out her kerchief and dipped the corner in the water and wiped her face. What had Vern told her? That she had to do what her heart tells her. (p. 99)

What Did You Notice?

We're sure you saw those important words "You gotta do what your heart tells you" again and again. That's because we found the three scenes in which they were repeated and placed them one after the other. That certainly made them easier to notice. But when you're reading a book on your own, you'll have to keep your eyes open for things that occur again and again.

Often, authors help us see the importance of Again and Again moments by repeating the words or phrases or events within a few pages or even a few sentences. Notice that the second time this phrase is used comes only two pages after the first time it was mentioned. The author really wants you to notice this! And when we see it a third time, some 59 pages later, the author helps us remember that this is an Again and Again moment by writing, "What had Vern told her?" Even if you can't remember the pages where you've seen this before, you now remember that you have.

Now, take a moment and jot down notes about why this advice from Vern might show up again and again.

_____

_____

_____

_____

_____

_____

Here's What We Noticed

From us both: We think these words are repeated because Charlotte must have some tough choices to make, and the advice of following her own heart will help her.

From Dr. Beers: Did you notice, also, that what is repeated is a Words of the Wiser lesson? That often happens with Words of the Wiser—the character keeps thinking about the advice, so it turns into an Again and Again signpost.

Quick Tip

Don't worry if you can't remember where you first saw a word or phrase in the book you're reading. Focus on why it keeps coming up again and again.

From Dr. Probst: And because the character keeps remembering the advice, then we also have a Memory Moment (see page 30).
It doesn't matter if you see these lines as a Memory Moment, Again and Again, or Words of the Wiser. What matters is that you see them and recognize that they are important and stop to think about what they mean.

Passage 2

Now read this passage, the first couple of paragraphs of *Maniac Magee*, by Jerry Spinelli. Underline what's repeated again and again and then ask yourself why this phrase would show up again and again.

> They say Maniac Magee was born in a dump. They say his stomach was a cereal box and his heart a sofa spring.
>
> They say he kept an eight-inch cockroach on a leash and that rats stood guard over him while he slept.
>
> They say if you knew he was coming and you sprinkled salt on the ground and he ran over it, within two or three blocks he would be as slow as everybody else.
>
> They say. (p. 1)

_____

_____

_____

_____

Here's What We Noticed

From both of us: When we read this, we immediately saw "they say" repeated in every sentence. This phrase is so important that the author ended this section with "They say." Now, _why would the author say this again and again?_ Well, we remembered when our kids would want to do something and would say to us, "They all get to do . . ." or "They all are going . . . ," and we would immediately ask, "Who is _they_?" And often, our kids didn't know! They were simply repeating something they had heard from other kids, or they didn't want to tell us the truth.

Ah! Our own Memory Moment!

We think the author is repeating "They say" to show us that people are all repeating things about Maniac that probably aren't true. As we keep reading, we'll keep in mind that some of the things we read in this book about Maniac might be rumor and some will be the truth. Distinguishing truth from rumor in this book will be important.

Quick Tip

The Again and Again signpost helps you recognize what is called "foreshadowing." Foreshadowing is a hint that authors give us about something that will happen later in a story. When your teacher asks you to look for foreshadowing, keep your eyes open for things that happen again and again.

STOP and Notice & Note

Memory Moment

When you're reading and the author interrupts the action to tell you a memory.

You should stop and ask yourself:

"Why might this memory be important?"

The answers will tell you about the theme, conflict or might foreshadow what will happen later in the story.

My Notes About
Memory Moment

_____

_____

_____

_____

_____

_____

_____

_____

_____

_____

_____

_____

_____

_____

_____

_____

_____

_____

_____

_____

_____

_____

_____

_____

Practice Noticing: **Memory Moment**

It's a rare day that something doesn't happen that reminds us of a moment from our pasts. One of us might recall a funny incident that happened with one of our kids. Or we might see or read something that reminds us of a book or a movie or an event from our own childhoods. And you saw the Memory Moment we had in the Again and Again section (see page 28). The point is, memories are a part of who we are, and when we share them, whoever we're with learns something new about us.

Authors help us understand characters in the same way, by sharing memories of things that have happened in the past. When you notice those memory moments, you need to stop and ask yourself, *Why might this memory be important?* You'll almost always discover that the memory helps you better understand a character's feelings or actions.

Take a look at the passages that follow to think about how memory moments help us learn about characters.

Passage 1

This passage is from *Hatchet*, by Gary Paulsen, a book about a boy named Brian who survives a plane crash and now finds himself alone in the Canadian wilderness. This is the second day after the crash, and he's just beginning to understand what it means to be alone with no supplies.

> There was nothing obvious to eat and aside from about a million birds and beaver he hadn't seen animals to trap and cook, and even if he got one somehow he didn't have any matches so he couldn't have a fire . . .
>   Nothing.
>   It kept coming back to that. He had nothing.
>   Well, almost nothing. As a matter of fact, he thought, I don't know what I've got or haven't got. Maybe I should try and figure out just how I stand. It will give me something to do.
>   Brian had once had an English teacher, a guy named Perpich, who was always talking about being positive, thinking positive, staying on top of things. That's how Perpich had put it—stay positive and stay on top of

things. Brian thought of him now—wondered how to stay positive and stay on top of this. (pp. 45–46)

What Did You Notice?

If you haven't already underlined the memory moment, reread the passage and do that. Then, in the blanks below, answer the anchor question, *Why might this memory be important?*

_____

_____

_____

_____

Here's What We Noticed

Brian had once had an English teacher, a guy named Perpich, who was always talking about being positive, thinking positive, staying on top of things. That's how Perpich had put it—stay positive and stay on top of things. Brian thought of him now—wondered how to stay positive and stay on top of this.

> This paragraph is the memory.

From Dr. Beers: In this passage, we see right away that the author is letting us in on a memory by just telling us "Brian had once had an English teacher. . . ." This memory is obviously important because in this desperate situation, Brian's first memory is a lesson he learned from his teacher. He doesn't share a memory about how to build a fire or catch a fish. Brian remembers how important a positive attitude is. That suggests to me that no matter what hardships Brian might face while stranded, staying positive is going to be the most important thing. It might even mean that this is what he will struggle with the most.

From Dr. Probst: I agree. And as I read this passage, I couldn't help but notice another signpost in this same memory moment. Read the entire passage again to see if you notice another signpost.

* * *

From Dr. Probst: The other signpost I saw was Tough Questions. Remember that tough questions may appear as "I wonder" statements. Here we see Brian wonder how he will stay positive. Tough questions show us the internal conflict. This is a survival book, which means we usually focus on how someone will survive with limited food and water, but after noticing this tough question, I realized that the real conflict will come from within. It will be about not giving up hope.

From Dr. Beers: And what I saw was a Words of the Wiser signpost. Mr. Perpich has given Brian some important advice. Remember, talking with your classmates about what you've each noticed gives you a chance to see the same passage in a new way."

Passage 2

Here's another Memory Moment. In this example, you might also notice some other signposts. Read the passage and underline all the signposts you notice, and then jot down your answers to the anchor questions for those signposts. This passage comes from a book titled *The Outsiders*, by S. E. Hinton. In this passage, Darry is relieved to discover that his brother Ponyboy is alive.

Quick Tip

Memory moments take us into someone's past, but as we think about them we realize we are learning something about the present or the future. Don't skip over these moments, because they often explain why the character acts or feels the way he does.

> He was stroking my hair and I could hear the sobs racking him as he fought to keep back the tears. "Oh, Pony, I thought we'd lost you . . . like we did Mom and Dad . . ."
>
> That was his silent fear then—of losing another person he loved. I remembered how close he and Dad had been, and I wondered how I could ever have thought him hard and unfeeling. (pp. 98–99)

_____

_____

_____

_____

_____

Here's What We Noticed

From both of us: We hope you easily noticed the phrase "I remembered how close he and Dad had been." That's an easy Memory Moment, and when you reflected on the importance of this moment, you probably wrote something about how this passage shows that Darry really misses his dad and that Ponyboy hadn't realized that.

Another Memory Moment is here, but it is a little more subtle. Darry says that he thought he had lost Ponyboy "like we did Mom and Dad." He doesn't say that he's remembering losing his mom and dad. He just compares something that's happening to something in the past, and we realize he's remembering his parents. Losing your parents is very difficult, so if he was comparing losing Ponyboy to losing his parents, then we realize how important Ponyboy is to him. That's why that memory is important to us, the readers. It reveals Darry's real feelings about Ponyboy.

> Each time you reread a short passage and think more about it, you are reading closely. You won't read an entire book this way, but it's important to read some passages with great intensity and attention.

Another signpost you might have noticed is Tough Questions. Did you see it? When Ponyboy says, "I wondered how I could have ever thought him hard and unfeeling," we understand something that has bothered Ponyboy. Remember that tough questions might appear as "I wonder" statements. Ponyboy wonders how he could have thought of Darry as hard and unfeeling. But because he states this in past tense—remember, he said "I wonder*ed*"—then we know that he isn't feeling this anymore. He now realizes that Darry loves him and so—aha—another signpost has just emerged! He realizes that Darry loves him even though Darry must have, at some point, acted hard and unfeeling. This one short passage shows us a lot about the relationship between these brothers.

Quick Tip

Memory moments are usually easy to spot because we see the words "I remembered" or "It came back to me" or "I recalled" or "I thought back to." If the main character is listening to someone else share a memory moment, you might read, "She told me about the time" or "We had to listen to stories from when she was little."

Part **Two**

My Reading Record

Why Keep a Reading Record?

Pilots keep a log of how many hours they have flown. Baseball players keep stats on how many hits they get and runs they score. Actors keep records of their starring roles. It's only natural, then, that readers keep a list of what they're reading. On the next two pages you will find a blank Reading Record to store the stats on some of your reading this year.

My Reading Record

Book Title and Author	Dates		Rate This Book
The Watsons Go to Birmingham—1963 by Christopher Paul Curtis	Started 9-25	Finished 10-12	☆ ☆ ☆ ☆ ☆ I love this book
Wonder by R. J Palacio	Started 11-13	Finished	
	Started	Finished	
	Started	Finished	
	Started	Finished	
	Started	Finished	
	Started	Finished	
	Started	Finished	
	Started	Finished	

Note names of books here.

Note when you began and finished here.

Draw how many stars you'd give this book and add a comment.

The Books I'm Reading

Book Title and Author	Dates		Rate This Book
	Started	Finished	
	Started	Finished	
	Started	Finished	
	Started	Finished	
	Started	Finished	
	Started	Finished	
	Started	Finished	
	Started	Finished	
	Started	Finished	
	Started	Finished	

My Reading Record

The Books I'm Reading

Book Title and Author	Dates		Rate This Book
	Started	Finished	
	Started	Finished	
	Started	Finished	
	Started	Finished	
	Started	Finished	
	Started	Finished	
	Started	Finished	
	Started	Finished	
	Started	Finished	
	Started	Finished	

My Reading Record

Part **Three**

My Book Notes

My Book Notes

In this section of your literature log, we've given you space to record your thinking about some of the books you read this year. This log has space for ten books. Some of you will read far more than that! If you do, just add more pages to this log, or ask your teacher for another one.

While we hope you'll use this section for recording your own thoughts, we know that it is often helpful to have some prompts about what to write. So in this section, you'll find nine pages per book for you to jot some notes. Several of the pages give you space to record the Notice and Note Signposts you've found. (We hope that doesn't surprise you!) Because we think this is a critical section, we thought it might be helpful to see a portion of one record from one student. This is from Madeline, and she's reading *The Giver*, by Lois Lowry.

Name Madeline   Class Period 3   Date Mar 16

Notice and Note Reading Log for *The Giver*

Location	Signpost I Noticed	My Notes About it
Page 2	Contrasts and contradictions	I noticed that everyone had to run just because a plane was flying and that isn't something I would do. It seemed like a Contrasts and contradictions lesson where something happens that seems odd. Maybe it was during a war and they were afraid this was a bomber.
Chapter 1	Again and Again	Release is used a lot and not as a good word. Jonas points out that he got punished for saying that Asher should be released.

> These are the notes you jot down about the signposts you spot.

Book 1: _____

Use these pages to keep notes about the signposts you've noticed.

Location	Signpost I Noticed	My Notes About It

My Book Notes

Book 1: _____

Location	Signpost I Noticed	My Notes About It

My Book Notes

Book 1: _____

Location	Signpost I Noticed	My Notes About It

My Book Notes

Book 1: _____

My thoughts or questions

Source or evidence from the book (page numbers or quoted passages)

> This is a student's comment from *The Watsons Go to Birmingham–1963*

Wow! Byron is really impressed
with himself!!

pp. 12–15: scene
where he kisses
himself

> And here is the evidence for that thought.

My Book Notes

Book 1: _____

My thoughts or questions	Source or evidence from the book (page numbers or quoted passages)
_____	_____
_____	_____
_____	_____
_____	_____
_____	_____
_____	_____
_____	_____
_____	_____
_____	_____
_____	_____
_____	_____
_____	_____
_____	_____
_____	_____
_____	_____
_____	_____
_____	_____
_____	_____
_____	_____
_____	_____
_____	_____
_____	_____

My Book Notes

Book 1: _____

Use this space to draw a favorite scence from the book or write summaries for various characters perhaps using the Somebody Wanted But So (SWBS) strategy.

Somebody	Wanted	But	So
Cinderella	to go to the ball	her stepmom said no	her fairy godmother helped her

My Book Notes

Book 1: _____

Use this space to draw a favorite scence from the book or write summaries for various characters perhaps using the Somebody Wanted But So (SWBS) strategy.

Book 1: _____

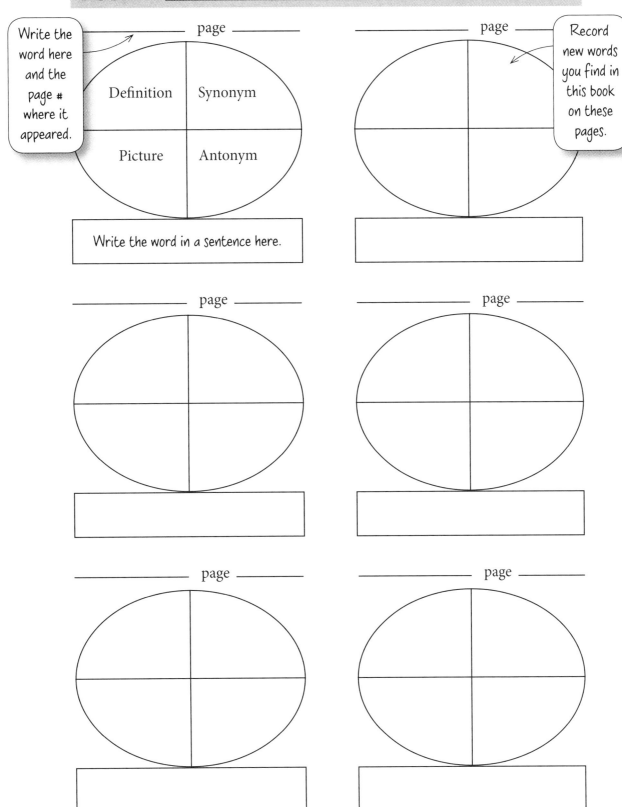

Write the word here and the page # where it appeared.

page _____

| Definition | Synonym |
| Picture | Antonym |

Write the word in a sentence here.

page _____

Record new words you find in this book on these pages.

page _____

page _____

page _____

page _____

My Book Notes

Book 1: _____

page _____   page _____

page _____   page _____

page _____   page _____

Book 2: _____

Use these pages to keep notes about the signposts you've noticed.

Location	Signpost I Noticed	My Notes About It

My Book Notes

Book 2: _____

Location	Signpost I Noticed	My Notes About It

My Book Notes

Book 2: _____

Location	Signpost I Noticed	My Notes About It

My Book Notes

Book 2: _____

My thoughts or questions	Source or evidence from the book (page numbers or quoted passages)

My Book Notes

Book 2: _____

My thoughts or questions	Source or evidence from the book (page numbers or quoted passages)
_____	_____
_____	_____
_____	_____
_____	_____
_____	_____
_____	_____
_____	_____
_____	_____
_____	_____
_____	_____
_____	_____
_____	_____
_____	_____
_____	_____
_____	_____
_____	_____
_____	_____
_____	_____
_____	_____
_____	_____
_____	_____
_____	_____

My Book Notes

Book 2: _____

Use this space to draw a favorite scence from the book or write summaries for various characters perhaps using the Somebody Wanted But So (SWBS) strategy.

© 2014 by Kylene Beers and Robert E. Probst from *Notice and Note Literature Log*. Portsmouth, NH: Heinemann.

Book 2: _____

Use this space to draw a favorite scence from the book or write summaries for various characters perhaps using the Somebody Wanted But So (SWBS) strategy.

58

Book 2: _____

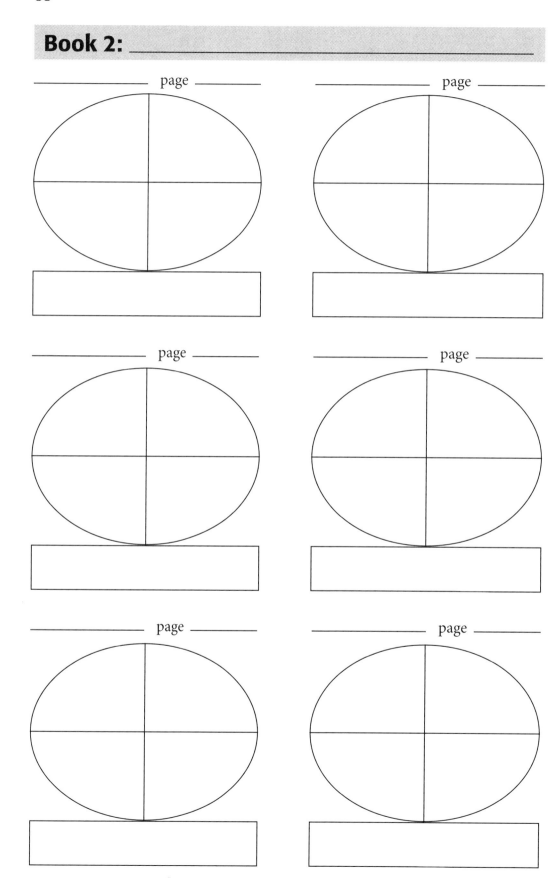

page _____   page _____

page _____   page _____

page _____   page _____

My Book Notes

Book 2: _____

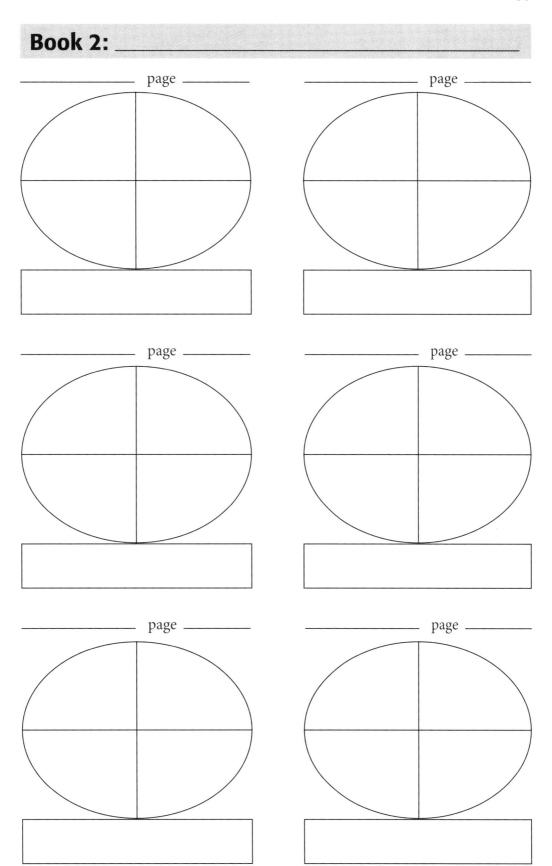

page _____   page _____

page _____   page _____

page _____   page _____

My Book Notes

Book 3: _____

Use these pages to keep notes about the signposts you've noticed.

Location	Signpost I Noticed	My Notes About It

My Book Notes

Book 3: _____

Location	Signpost I Noticed	My Notes About It

My Book Notes

Book 3: _____

Location	Signpost I Noticed	My Notes About It

My Book Notes

Book 3: _____

My thoughts or questions	Source or evidence from the book (page numbers or quoted passages)

My Book Notes

Book 3: _____

My thoughts or questions	Source or evidence from the book (page numbers or quoted passages)

My Book Notes

Book 3: _____

Use this space to draw a favorite scence from the book or write summaries for various characters perhaps using the Somebody Wanted But So (SWBS) strategy.

My Book Notes

Book 3: _____

Use this space to draw a favorite scence from the book or write summaries for various characters perhaps using the Somebody Wanted But So (SWBS) strategy.

© 2014 by Kylene Beers and Robert E. Probst from *Notice and Note Literature Log*. Portsmouth, NH: Heinemann.

My Book Notes

Book 3: _____

page _____

page _____

page _____

page _____

page _____

page _____

68

Book 3: _____

_____ page _____

_____ page _____

_____ page _____

_____ page _____

_____ page _____

_____ page _____

Book 4: _____

Use these pages to keep notes about the signposts you've noticed.

Location	Signpost I Noticed	My Notes About It

My Book Notes

Book 4: _____

Location	Signpost I Noticed	My Notes About It

My Book Notes

Book 4: _____

Location	Signpost I Noticed	My Notes About It

My Book Notes

Book 4: _____

My thoughts or questions	Source or evidence from the book (page numbers or quoted passages)
_____	_____
_____	_____
_____	_____
_____	_____
_____	_____
_____	_____
_____	_____
_____	_____
_____	_____
_____	_____
_____	_____
_____	_____
_____	_____
_____	_____
_____	_____
_____	_____
_____	_____
_____	_____
_____	_____
_____	_____

My Book Notes

Book 4: _____

My thoughts or questions	Source or evidence from the book (page numbers or quoted passages)

My Book Notes

Book 4: _____

Use this space to draw a favorite scence from the book or write summaries for various characters perhaps using the Somebody Wanted But So (SWBS) strategy.

My Book Notes

Book 4: _____

Use this space to draw a favorite scence from the book or write summaries for various characters perhaps using the Somebody Wanted But So (SWBS) strategy.

Book 4: _____

_____ page _____

_____ page _____

_____ page _____

_____ page _____

_____ page _____

_____ page _____

My Book Notes

Book 4: _____

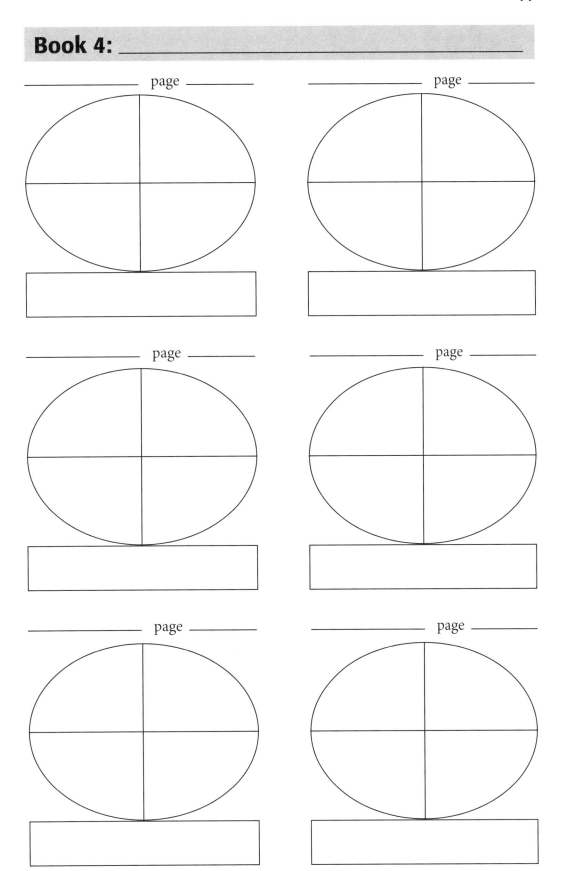

page _____	page _____
page _____	page _____
page _____	page _____

My Book Notes

Book 5: _____

Use these pages to keep notes about the signposts you've noticed.

Location	Signpost I Noticed	My Notes About It

My Book Notes

Book 5: _____

Location	Signpost I Noticed	My Notes About It

My Book Notes

Book 5: _____

Location	Signpost I Noticed	My Notes About It

My Book Notes

Book 5: _____

My thoughts or questions	Source or evidence from the book (page numbers or quoted passages)

My Book Notes

Book 5: _____

My thoughts or questions	Source or evidence from the book (page numbers or quoted passages)
_____	_____
_____	_____
_____	_____
_____	_____
_____	_____
_____	_____
_____	_____
_____	_____
_____	_____
_____	_____
_____	_____
_____	_____
_____	_____
_____	_____
_____	_____
_____	_____
_____	_____
_____	_____
_____	_____
_____	_____

My Book Notes

Book 5: _____

Use this space to draw a favorite scence from the book or write summaries for various characters perhaps using the Somebody Wanted But So (SWBS) strategy.

My Book Notes

Book 5: _____

Use this space to draw a favorite scence from the book or write summaries for various characters perhaps using the Somebody Wanted But So (SWBS) strategy.

© 2014 by Kylene Beers and Robert E. Probst from *Notice and Note Literature Log*. Portsmouth, NH: Heinemann.

Book 5: _____

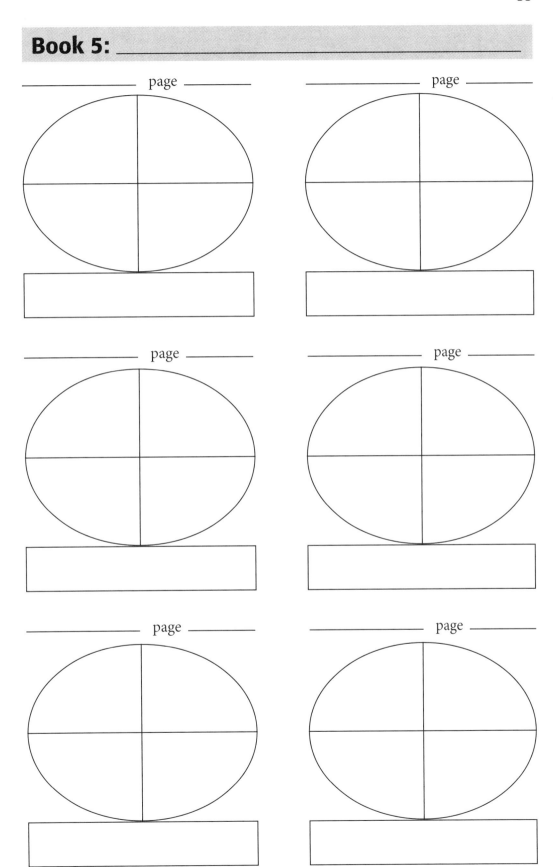

page _____   page _____

page _____   page _____

page _____   page _____

My Book Notes

Book 5: _____

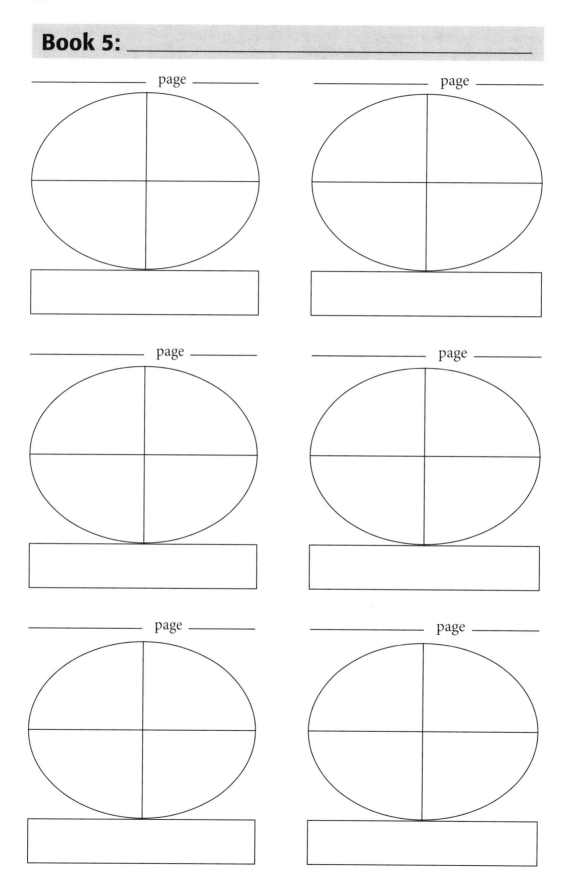

page _____

page _____

page _____

page _____

page _____

page _____

My Book Notes

Book 6: _____

Use these pages to keep notes about the signposts you've noticed.

Location	Signpost I Noticed	My Notes About It

My Book Notes

Book 6: _____

Location	Signpost I Noticed	My Notes About It

My Book Notes

Book 6: _____

Location	Signpost I Noticed	My Notes About It

My Book Notes

Book 6: _____

My thoughts or questions	Source or evidence from the book (page numbers or quoted passages)

My Book Notes

Book 6: _____

My thoughts or questions	Source or evidence from the book (page numbers or quoted passages)

My Book Notes

Book 6: _____

Use this space to draw a favorite scence from the book or write summaries for various characters perhaps using the Somebody Wanted But So (SWBS) strategy.

Book 6: _____

Use this space to draw a favorite scence from the book or write summaries for various characters perhaps using the Somebody Wanted But So (SWBS) strategy.

My Book Notes

Book 6: _____

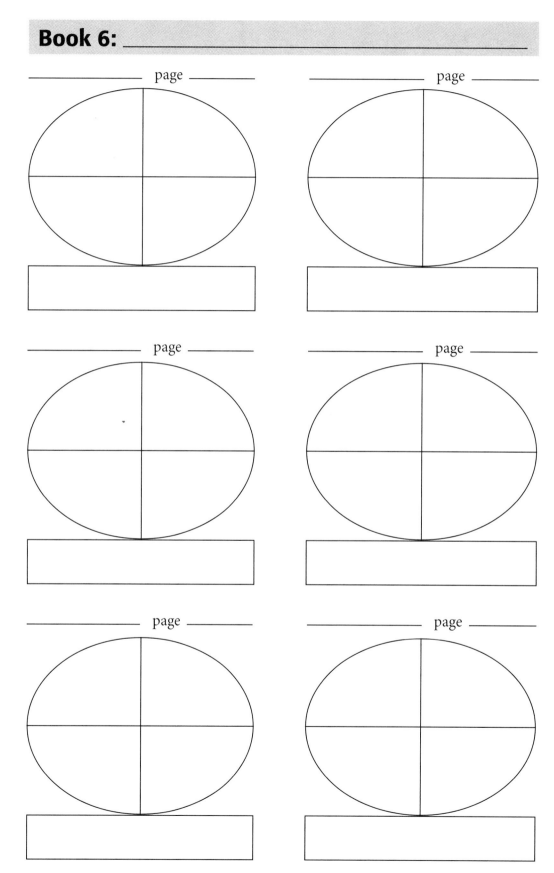

page _____ _____

page _____ _____

page _____ _____

page _____ _____

page _____ _____

page _____ _____

My Book Notes

Book 6: _____

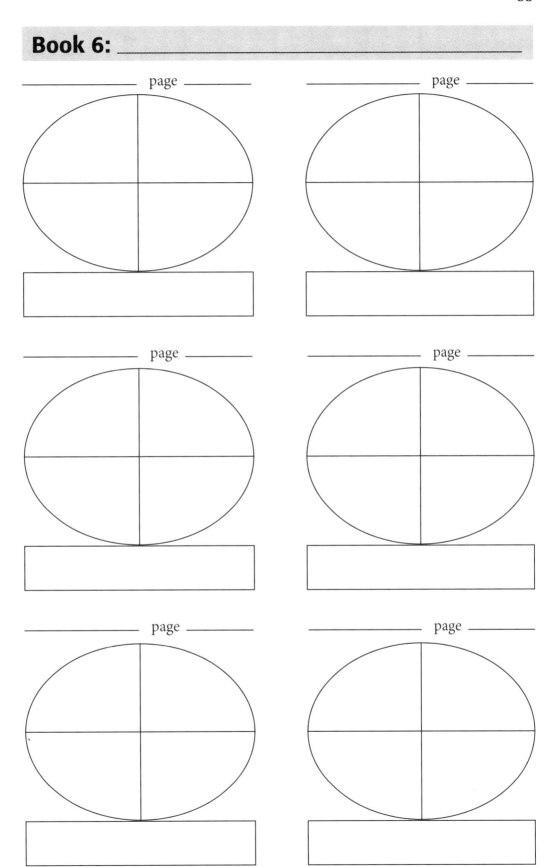

page _____

page _____

page _____

page _____

page _____

page _____

My Book Notes

Book 7: _____

Use these pages to keep notes about the signposts you've noticed.

Location	Signpost I Noticed	My Notes About It

My Book Notes

Book 7: _____

Location	Signpost I Noticed	My Notes About It

My Book Notes

Book 7: _____

Location	Signpost I Noticed	My Notes About It

My Book Notes

Book 7: _____

My thoughts or questions	Source or evidence from the book (page numbers or quoted passages)

My Book Notes

Book 7: _____

My thoughts or questions	Source or evidence from the book (page numbers or quoted passages)
_____	_____
_____	_____
_____	_____
_____	_____
_____	_____
_____	_____
_____	_____
_____	_____
_____	_____
_____	_____
_____	_____
_____	_____
_____	_____
_____	_____
_____	_____
_____	_____
_____	_____
_____	_____
_____	_____
_____	_____

My Book Notes

Book 7: _____

Use this space to draw a favorite scence from the book or write summaries for various characters perhaps using the Somebody Wanted But So (SWBS) strategy.

Book 7: _____

Use this space to draw a favorite scence from the book or write summaries for various characters perhaps using the Somebody Wanted But So (SWBS) strategy.

© 2014 by Kylene Beers and Robert E. Probst from *Notice and Note Literature Log*. Portsmouth, NH: Heinemann.

Book 7: _____

——— page ———

——— page ———

——— page ———

——— page ———

——— page ———

——— page ———

My Book Notes

Book 7: _____

_____ page _____

_____ page _____

_____ page _____

_____ page _____

_____ page _____

_____ page _____

Book 8: _____

Use these pages to keep notes about the signposts you've noticed.

Location	Signpost I Noticed	My Notes About It

My Book Notes

Book 8: _____

Location	Signpost I Noticed	My Notes About It

My Book Notes

Book 8: _____

Location	Signpost I Noticed	My Notes About It

My Book Notes

Book 8: _____

My thoughts or questions	Source or evidence from the book (page numbers or quoted passages)

My Book Notes

Book 8: _____

My thoughts or questions	Source or evidence from the book (page numbers or quoted passages)
_____	_____
_____	_____
_____	_____
_____	_____
_____	_____
_____	_____
_____	_____
_____	_____
_____	_____
_____	_____
_____	_____
_____	_____
_____	_____
_____	_____
_____	_____
_____	_____
_____	_____
_____	_____
_____	_____
_____	_____
_____	_____

My Book Notes

Book 8: _____

Use this space to draw a favorite scence from the book or write summaries for various characters perhaps using the Somebody Wanted But So (SWBS) strategy.

My Book Notes

Book 8: _____

Use this space to draw a favorite scence from the book or write summaries for various characters perhaps using the Somebody Wanted But So (SWBS) strategy.

© 2014 by Kylene Beers and Robert E. Probst from *Notice and Note Literature Log*. Portsmouth, NH: Heinemann.

Book 8: _____

——— page ———

——— page ———

——— page ———

——— page ———

——— page ———

——— page ———

Book 8: _____

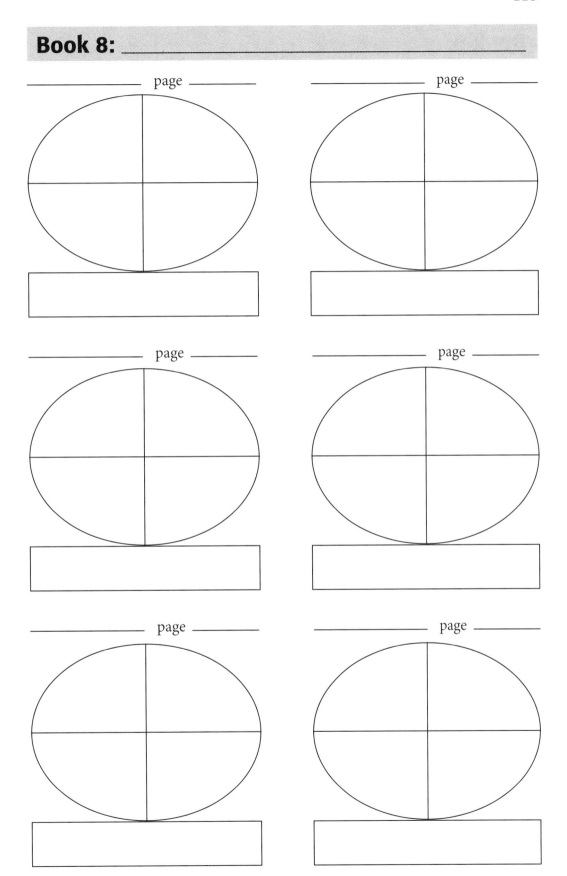

page _____

page _____

page _____

page _____

page _____

page _____

Book 9: _____

Use these pages to keep notes about the signposts you've noticed.

Location	Signpost I Noticed	My Notes About It

My Book Notes

Book 9: _____

Location	Signpost I Noticed	My Notes About It

My Book Notes

Book 9: _____

Location	Signpost I Noticed	My Notes About It

Book 9: _____

My thoughts or questions	Source or evidence from the book (page numbers or quoted passages)

My Book Notes

Book 9: _____

My thoughts or questions	Source or evidence from the book (page numbers or quoted passages)

Book 9: _____

Use this space to draw a favorite scence from the book or write summaries for various characters perhaps using the Somebody Wanted But So (SWBS) strategy.

Book 9: _____

Use this space to draw a favorite scence from the book or write summaries for various characters perhaps using the Somebody Wanted But So (SWBS) strategy.

Book 9: _____

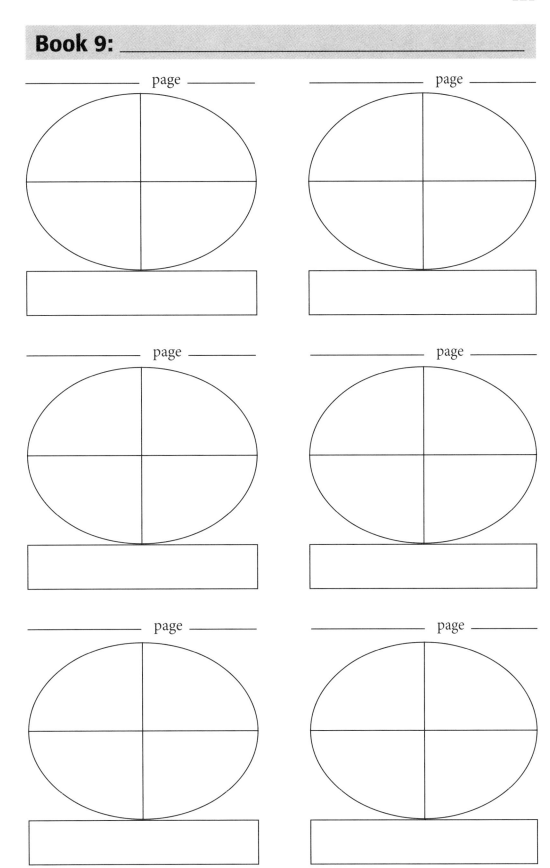

page _____   page _____

page _____   page _____

page _____   page _____

My Book Notes

Book 9: _____

_____ page _____

_____ page _____

_____ page _____

_____ page _____

_____ page _____

_____ page _____

Book 10: _____

Use these pages to keep notes about the signposts you've noticed.

Location	Signpost I Noticed	My Notes About It

My Book Notes

Book 10: _____

Location	Signpost I Noticed	My Notes About It

My Book Notes

Book 10: _____

Location	Signpost I Noticed	My Notes About It

My Book Notes

Book 10: _____

My thoughts or questions	Source or evidence from the book (page numbers or quoted passages)
_____	_____
_____	_____
_____	_____
_____	_____
_____	_____
_____	_____
_____	_____
_____	_____
_____	_____
_____	_____
_____	_____
_____	_____
_____	_____
_____	_____
_____	_____
_____	_____
_____	_____
_____	_____
_____	_____
_____	_____

My Book Notes

Book 10: _____

My thoughts or questions	Source or evidence from the book (page numbers or quoted passages)

My Book Notes

Book 10: _____

Use this space to draw a favorite scence from the book or write summaries for various characters perhaps using the Somebody Wanted But So (SWBS) strategy.

My Book Notes

Book 10: _____

Use this space to draw a favorite scence from the book or write summaries for various characters perhaps using the Somebody Wanted But So (SWBS) strategy.

Book 10: _____

_____ page _____

_____ page _____

_____ page _____

_____ page _____

_____ page _____

_____ page _____

Book 10: _____

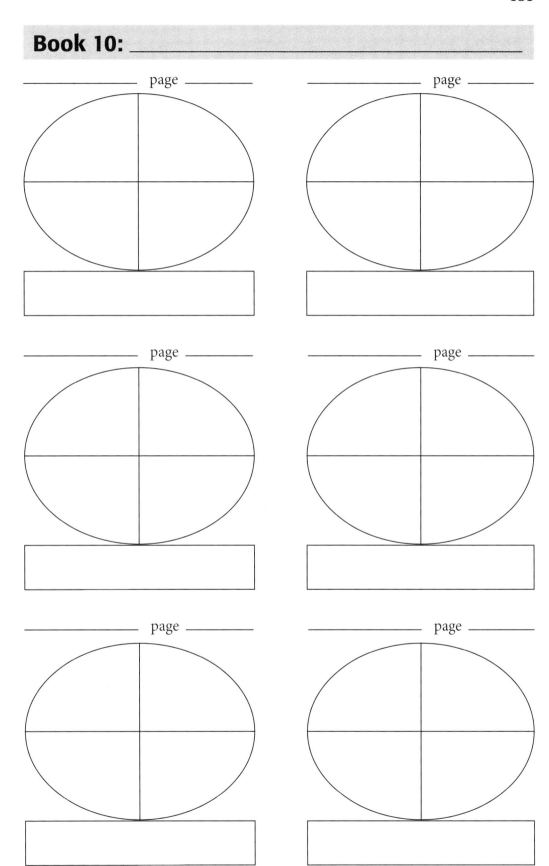

page ———————   page ———————

page ———————   page ———————

page ———————   page ———————

My Book Notes

Notes

Notes

Notes

Notes

Notes